Pupil's Book 6

CB030999

Welcome Back to Quest TV!
page 2

1 Focus on Free Time
page 5

5 Where Were You?
page 37

Everyday English — page 12

Everyday English — page 44

2 Fashion Fix
page 13

6 Eureka!
page 45

Everyday English — page 20

Everyday English — page 52

3 Marvellous Myths
page 21

7 On Safari
page 53

Everyday English — page 28

Everyday English — page 60

4 Let's Cook!
page 29

8 Party Time!
page 61

Everyday English — page 36

Everyday English — page 68

Festivals
page 69

Emma Mohamed

Welcome Back to Quest TV!

Quest TV Studio

Lessons 1 and 2

1 **Listen and point.**

Hi everyone! Welcome back to Quest TV, your favourite TV show! I'm Kiera, and here we are in our new Quest TV studio. And the studio isn't the only new thing. It looks like Dan has got a new laptop.

Yes, I have! It's great and it's very fast! And Kiera, I love your new sunglasses. They're cool!

2  **Find. Listen and check.**

| 1 a fruit | 2 a vegetable | 3 a type of transport | 4 the opposite of 'serious' | 5 a job |
| 6 a sport | 7 a country | 8 an item of clothing | 9 a place to visit | 10 an animal |

3 🎧 1/4 Read and match. Listen and check.

1 How many brothers and sisters have you got?
2 When's your birthday?
3 Who's your favourite actor?
4 Where do you live?
5 What's your favourite food?

a Penelope Cruz
b pizza
c in London
d three
e in November

Do you like my new bag, Jack? It's a pink sports bag! I love sport!

I love your new bag, Sophie. And look, this is my new T-shirt. It's got an octopus on it. It's my favourite animal!

4 🎧 1/5 Listen and read. Sing the song.

Welcome back to Quest TV,
The best TV show that you can see.
Here's the Quest team, oh yes, they're back!
It's Kiera, Dan, Sophie and Jack!

New stories to read, more songs to sing.
You can learn lots more English with Quest TV.
New words to learn, more grammar to do.
Quest is fun and it's ready for you!

Welcome back to Quest TV,
The best TV show that you can see!
Here's the Quest team, oh yes, they're back!
It's Kiera, Dan, Sophie and Jack!

Lesson 3

Quest TV Studio

1 Read and match.

Ask the audience!

What time do you …
1 get up on Saturday?
2 have Sunday lunch?
3 tidy your room?
4 play computer games?
5 study English?
6 do your homework?
7 visit friends or family?
8 go to bed?

2 **Listen and read. Ask and answer.**

What time do you …?

I always study English at quarter past three on Monday.

I often visit my grandma after school.

I do my homework at five o'clock.

I sometimes go to bed at half past nine.

   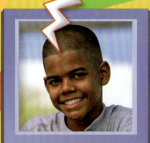 

3 **Put the times in order. Listen and check.**

TO   PAST

half past six
five past six
twenty to six
ten to six
twenty-five past six
quarter past six

quarter to six
ten past six
five to six
twenty-five to six
twenty past six
six o'clock

It's twenty-five to six.

4

Focus on Free Time

Lesson 1

1 **Listen and repeat the words.**

Word Quest 1

1 play table tennis

2 play the drums

3 paint pictures

4 paint models

5 collect stickers

6 collect stamps

7 go fishing

8 go to the cinema

9 do magic tricks

10 do exercise

2 **Quest Memory Game. Listen and play.**

3 **Listen and read. Sing the song.**

Monday to Friday, it's school every day.
I'm with all my friends, so I feel ok.
On Tuesday, we paint models after school.
We collect stickers, too – it's really cool!

But on Saturday,
I'm free!
I play the drums all day,
Come and listen to me!
And on Sunday,
I'm free!
I want to be a pop star,
Come and listen to me!

Monday to Friday, it's school every day.
I'm with all my friends, so I feel ok.
On Wednesday, we go fishing after school.
We go to the cinema, too – it's really cool!

Chorus

Lesson 2

4 Listen to the story. Read.

See what happens when a young boy starts painting pictures on holiday with his family!

The Young Picasso

1. Kieron is five years old and he lives with his family in England. He likes going fishing and he loves playing football.

Look Dad! I've got a fish.

That's great, Kieron.

2. One day on holiday, Kieron starts painting pictures.

That's a really good picture, Kieron.

Thanks Mum. I like painting boats.

3. After his holiday, Kieron goes to painting classes. There aren't any children in the class, but that's ok for Kieron.

You can add some white paint here.

That's a good idea. Thanks.

4. Kieron doesn't like painting with children's paints. He paints pictures of people's pets for money to help him buy professional paints.

Here's the picture of your dog.

Thanks Kieron. It's fantastic!

5. Kieron paints lots of pictures. He's very good.

Hello! Can I have some paints, please?

Of course! Here you are.

6. Soon Kieron is in the newspapers and on TV.

Does Kieron like painting boats?

Yes, he does.

And I like painting landscapes and animals.

7. This is Kieron at his first art exhibition. People from all over the world want to buy his pictures.

A boy of seven sells all his pictures in fourteen minutes.

Kieron Williamson is an excellent artist.

England's Young Artist!

Some people call Kieron Williamson a mini Monet or a mini Picasso because he paints beautiful pictures and he's only a young boy. Some of his pictures cost thousands of pounds. He's very famous.

Lesson 3

5 Let's investigate grammar.

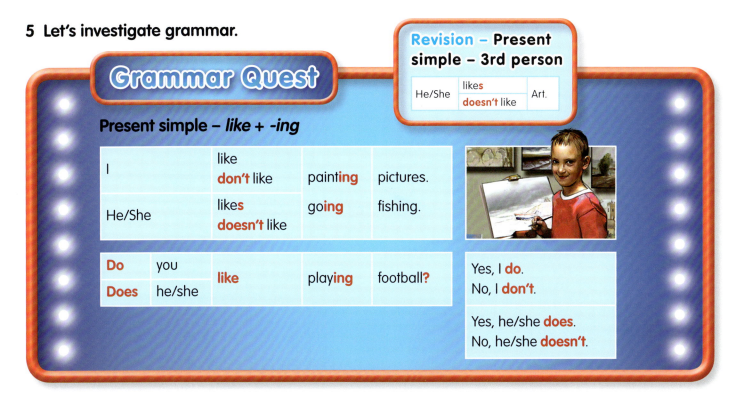

6 Answer the questions. Look at the Grammar Quest to help you.

1 Do we use the verb **with** or **without** *-ing* after **like**/**likes**?
2 Do we use the verb **with** or **without** *-ing* after **don't like**/**doesn't like**?
3 Do we start the **question** for **he**/**she** with **Does** or **Do**?

7 Listen, read and repeat. Act it out.

An interview with *Free Time Magazine*

Interviewer: What do the Quest team do in their free time?
Jack: Well, Sophie loves sport.
Interviewer: Oh yes. What's her favourite sport?
Jack: She loves playing table tennis. And she's very good.
Interviewer: And what about Dan?
Jack: He likes going to the cinema.
Interviewer: Does Kiera like going to the cinema, too?
Jack: Yes, she does. And she likes collecting stamps.
Interviewer: And do you like collecting stamps, Jack?
Jack: No, I don't. I love doing magic tricks. Look!
Interviewer: Oh, what lovely flowers! Thank you!

Lesson 4

8 Listen and repeat the words.

Word Quest 2

1 a paintbrush   2 an album   3 an exercise mat   4 a pack of cards   5 a fishing rod

9 Listen and read. Answer the question.

Text type: a web page

Which 3 hobbies are in the texts?

Hobbies

are a great way to learn something new and to have fun. There are lots of different hobbies. Here are some of the hobbies you can do:

Doing magic tricks is a cool hobby. The formula 1 driver, Fernando Alonso, loves doing card tricks! All you need is a pack of cards and some instructions. And you need to practise. Then you can do your card or other magic tricks for people!

Collecting stamps is an interesting hobby. You can take the stamps from old letters and postcards. It's a good idea to buy an album. You can organise your stamp collection by theme, like putting all your animal stamps together. John Lennon's stamp collection is in a museum!

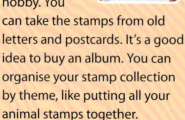

Doing exercise is a good hobby and it's healthy. You need an exercise mat and comfortable clothes. You can do exercise wherever you want – in your bedroom, in the garden or even on the beach! The pop star, Shakira, does lots of exercise. She likes dancing, too!

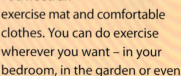

What equipment do you need for your favourite hobby?

10 Listen and answer the questions you hear. Listen and check.

11 Listen and say.

Funky Phonics

People's hobbies, people's hobbies.
What hobbies do they do?
They put stamps in albums, play table tennis,
And paint pictures with paintbrushes, too!

1 Lesson 5 CLIL Art

12 Listen and read. Answer the audience questions.

CONTEMPORARY ARTISTS

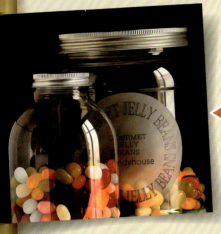

Audience Questions:
1 Where is the artist Pedro Campos from?
SMS from Sarah in England
2 What style of Art is Julian Opie famous for?
SMS from Mark in Scotland
3 What does Julian Opie like painting?
SMS from Eleri in Wales
4 What style of Art is Frank Stella famous for?
SMS from Brian in Ireland

◄ Pedro Campos
He's an artist from Spain. He was born in 1966. He studied at an Art restoration school in Madrid. He's famous for his 'hyperrealist' style of art. He likes painting everyday objects, for example apples, cans of cola and sweets. His paintings look very realistic, like photographs.

Julian Opie ►
He's an artist from England. He was born in 1958. He studied at an Art school in London. He's famous for his popular style of art, or 'pop art'. He likes painting people. His paintings look very simple. They don't have a lot of detail. He painted a CD cover for a famous British band called Blur.

Amazing fact
Julian Opie designed a stamp for the London 2012 Olympics.

◄ Frank Stella
He's an artist from the USA. He was born in 1936. He studied painting at Phillips Academy in Massachusetts. He's famous for his 'minimalist' style of art. He likes painting straight lines and curved lines. Colours and shapes are important in his paintings. He also likes making sculptures. He thinks sculptures are like three-dimensional (3D) paintings.

Amazing fact
Frank Stella sometimes uses normal house paint.

13 Read and say 'True' or 'False'.
1 Lots of Pedro Campos' paintings look like photographs.
2 Julian Opie painted a CD cover.
3 Frank Stella is from the UK.
4 Frank Stella likes painting people.

 Online Quest What style of art was the artist Andy Warhol famous for?

Lesson 6

Culture Quiz

14 **Do the quiz. Listen and check.**

1. The most popular day for going shopping in the UK is on … .
   a) Monday   b) Thursday   c) Saturday

2. People in the UK spend about half their free time … .
   a) watching TV   b) playing the drums   c) going fishing

3. The first world table tennis championship was in … .
   a) Dublin   b) Edinburgh   c) London

4. The first stamps were from … in 1840.
   a) the USA   b) the UK   c) Australia

5. In the USA, … is one of the most popular hobbies.
   a) doing exercise   b) painting models   c) collecting stamps

Language fact
In the UK, people often say 'Enjoy yourself!' or 'Have fun!' when they want someone to like an activity.

15 **Listen and read.**

Star Writer

Write to Quest TV.
Tell us about what you and your friend do in your free time.

Dear Quest team,

My name's Jim. In my free time I like going to the cinema. My favourite films are adventure films. I also like doing magic tricks. I normally use a pack of cards and do magic tricks for my sister and my friends. I don't like painting pictures. My friend's name is Diana and she loves painting pictures. She loves playing the drums, too. She's really good! She likes doing exercise, but she doesn't like going to the cinema. She likes my magic tricks!

Bye, Jim

Lesson 7:
Write your letter (Activity Book, page 11).

Lesson 8:
Do the Progress Check (Activity Book, page 12).

Unit 1 Language Guide

Word Quest 1

 1 play table tennis
 2 paint pictures
 3 collect stickers
 4 go fishing
 5 do magic tricks

 6 play the drums
 7 paint models
 8 collect stamps
 9 go to the cinema
 10 do exercise

Word Quest 2

 1 a paintbrush
 2 an album
 3 an exercise mat
 4 a pack of cards
 5 a fishing rod

 Go to the Bilingual Dictionary (Activity Book, page 14). **45 words and expressions**

Grammar Quest

Present simple – *like* + *-ing*

Affirmative and negative

I / You	like / **don't** like	paint**ing** go**ing**	pictures. fishing.
He/She	like**s** / **doesn't** like		
We / You / They	like / **don't** like		

Questions and short answers

Do you / **Does** he/she	**like** play**ing** football**?**

Yes, I **do**. No, I **don't**.	Yes, he/she **does**. No, he/she **doesn't**.

Remember!
He like**s** painting pictures.
She **doesn't** like going fishing.

 Go to Unit 1 in your Grammar Builder.

Everyday English

1 **LISTENING** Listen and answer the questions.

   1 Which picture is it – A or B?
   2 What type of stickers are the children collecting?
   3 What's the name of the boy playing table tennis?

FREE TIME AT THE PARK

2 **SPEAKING** Talk with a partner. How are pictures A and B different?

> In picture A, the girl doesn't like painting pictures.

> In picture B, the girl likes painting pictures.

3 Listen, read and repeat. Act it out.

- What's wrong, James?
- **I'm bored!**
- **Let's** paint a picture.
- No, I don't want to. I don't like painting.
- **Let's** watch TV.
- No, I don't want to.
- I know. **Let's** go to the park.
- Go to the park? Can we play table tennis?
- Yes, ok.
- Yippee! **I'm not bored** anymore!
- Oh good!

Fashion Fix

Lesson 1

1 **Listen and repeat the words.**

Word Quest 1

 1 sandals
 2 a cap
 3 a polo shirt
 4 shorts
 5 a tracksuit
 6 a denim skirt
 7 leggings
 8 trousers
 9 a headband
 10 a necklace

2 **Quest Memory Game. Listen and play.**

3 **Listen and read. Sing the song.**

He's wearing black trousers and a polo shirt.
She's wearing silver sandals
And a denim skirt.
They feel good, walking down the street.
They're all dressed up, from head to feet.

Everyone's looking at them,
Yes, they are!
Because they're wearing
cool clothes.
Yes, they're fashion stars!

She's wearing grey leggings
And a necklace that's red.
He's wearing shorts
And a cap on his head.
They look happy, walking along.
They're all dressed up, they can't go wrong.

Chorus

Lesson 2

4 🎧 **Listen to the story. Read.**

The Fashion Show

See what happens when Greenhill school has its very own fashion show!

1 Every year at Greenhill school, there's a fashion show.

GREENHILL FASHION SHOW
You can be a model in the show, or you can help design the clothes. Look different and use your **imagination**. Win the fashion show and be Greenhill school's fashion star!

2 It's a week before the fashion show. The children are at school.

Maybe I can win.

Don't be silly, Sandra. I'm the fashion star! I always wear great clothes.

I can help you, Sandra.

3 Sandra often does her homework with Dave. But today she isn't doing her homework …

Look at these great things! Now, where's your denim skirt?

Here. Wow, there are necklaces, flowers and stars!

4 Sandra and Dave leave the Art room.

Look! Sandra's clothes are good.

Not any more! She can't win the fashion show now. Ha, ha!

5 Sandra and Dave come back into the Art room.

Oh no! Dave, look at my skirt! I can't win now.

Don't worry, Sandra. I've got an idea. Where are your leggings?

6 A few days later, at the fashion show …

And here's last year's winner, Cassy.

She's wearing a fantastic long dress, silver sandals and a silver headband.

7 At last, it's Sandra's big moment …

And here's Sandra. She's wearing a necklace, a denim skirt and leggings. Look at all those colours!

8 And the winner is … Sandra! For such colourful and imaginative clothes.

Thank you everyone. And thank you Dave. He's got great ideas and he always helps me!

Lesson 3

5 Let's investigate grammar.

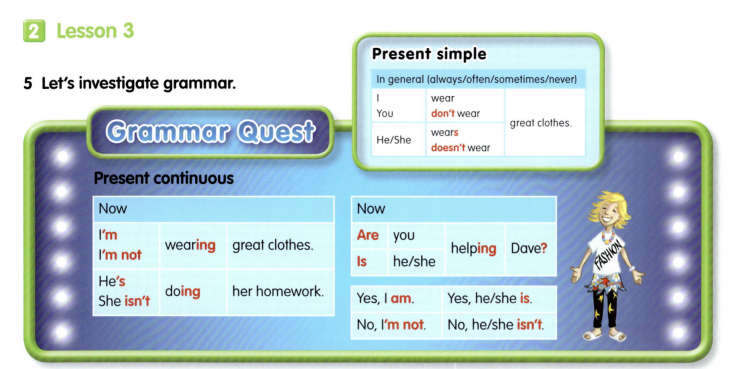

6 Answer the questions. Look at the Grammar Quest to help you.

1 When we talk about things **in general**, do we use the **present simple** or the **present continuous**?
2 Do we use **be + verb + -ing** when we talk about things **in general** or **now**?
3 Do we use **don't**/**doesn't** with the **present simple** or the **present continuous**?

7 Listen, read and repeat. Act it out.

The Quest TV Fashion Show

Dan: Today our show is about fashion.
Sophie: I often wear a T-shirt and trousers.
Dan: But today Sophie is wearing a denim skirt and grey leggings.
Sophie: And look at Dan. What's he wearing? Dan sometimes wears a polo shirt, but today he's wearing a blue T-shirt with shorts and a red cap.
Dan: And Sophie is wearing a necklace. She never wears necklaces!
Sophie: I know! I like what I'm wearing today. What about you, Dan?
Dan: Er, I'm not sure!

2 Lesson 4

8 Listen and repeat the words.

Word Quest 2

1 cotton 2 wool 3 silk 4 denim 5 leather

9 Listen and read. Answer the question.

Text type: **an advertisement**

Which material isn't in the text?

FUNKY CLOTHES

THE BEST CLOTHES SHOP IN TOWN!

Mix and match different materials. Look at our models and see how to do it!

- He's wearing a black leather jacket and a white cotton T-shirt.
- He's wearing black denim jeans. He looks cool!

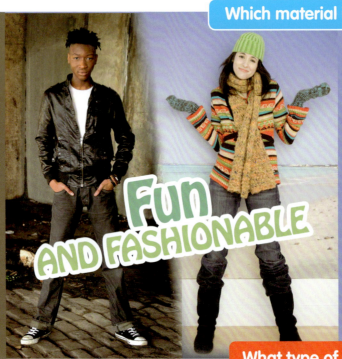

Fun AND FASHIONABLE

- She's wearing lots of wool. Her hat, scarf, gloves and jumper are all made of wool. She looks warm.
- She's wearing blue denim jeans and boots, too.

COME TO **FUNKY CLOTHES**

YOU CAN LOOK FUN AND FASHIONABLE, TOO!

What type of clothes do you prefer?

10 Listen and answer the questions you hear. Listen and check.

11 Listen and say.

Winter gloves, winter gloves.
White woolly winter gloves.
Vera's very white
woolly winter gloves.
Will's wearing Vera's very white
woolly winter gloves!

2 Lesson 5 CLIL Science

12 Listen and read. Answer the audience questions.

Where materials come from

Cotton is a natural material. It comes from cotton plants. The cotton plants go to a textile mill where machines clean the cotton. Later, other machines spin the cotton into strands. Then, machines weave the strands into cloth.

This is the pop star, Katy Perry. What's she wearing?

a cotton and nylon dress
Cotton is cool when it's hot! Nylon is strong and elastic.

a woolly cardigan
Wool is warm and light to wear.

leather shoes
Leather lasts a long time!

Nylon is an artificial material. It's a type of plastic. Nylon is made in a chemical plant. Machines mix chemicals at a high temperature to make a semi liquid. Later, other machines spin this semi liquid into strands of nylon. Then, machines weave the strands into cloth.

Audience Questions:
1 Where does cotton come from?
SMS from Paula in Wales
2 Is nylon a natural material?
SMS from Ben in England
3 Where do people make nylon?
SMS from Jenny in Scotland
4 Which material comes from animal skin?
SMS from Kieron in Ireland

Amazing fact
Prehistoric cave paintings show people wearing leather clothes – that's how old leather is!

Amazing fact
The money in the USA isn't made of paper, it's 75% cotton!

Amazing fact
Some people say that the word nylon comes from New York and London!

Leather is a natural material. It comes from the skin of animals, especially cows. The animal skins go to a tannery. Here, different chemicals make the animal skins into leather. Some chemicals clean the leather, some chemicals preserve it, and some chemicals make the leather hard or soft.

13 Read and say 'True' or 'False'.
1 Cotton is an artificial material.
2 Nylon is a type of plastic.
3 People make cotton in a tannery.
4 Leather can be hard or soft.

 Where does linen come from?

2 Lesson 6

Culture Quiz

14 Do the quiz. Listen and check.

1. A kilt is a traditional ... for men from Scotland.
   a) polo shirt   b) skirt   c) tracksuit

2. The miniskirt comes from ... .
   a) the UK   b) the USA   c) Canada

3. Jeans are made from a material called denim. Denim is a type of ... .
   a) wool   b) leather   c) cotton

4. ... is a city in the USA famous for fashion.
   a) New York   b) New Orleans   c) Las Vegas

5. Silk is a material that comes from ... .
   a) a plant   b) a bird   c) a worm

the USA

the UK

Language fact

In the UK, people often say 'What a great T-shirt!' or 'What great shoes!' when they really like your clothes.

15 Listen and read.

Star Writer

Write to Quest TV.
Tell us about your clothes. Tell us about a friend's clothes, too.

Hi Quest team,

Today I'm wearing black leggings, a white T-shirt and red trainers. My T-shirt has got a heart on it. At the weekend, I often wear my favourite denim skirt and my blue leggings – I think it looks cool! I sometimes wear jeans, but I don't often wear a dress.
My friend is called Jane. Today she's wearing denim shorts, a cotton T-shirt, a cap and brown leather sandals.

See you!
Emma

Jane and me

Lesson 7:
Write your letter (Activity Book, page 21).

Lesson 8:
Do the Progress Check (Activity Book, page 22).

Unit 2 Language Guide

Word Quest 1

1 sandals

2 a cap

3 a polo shirt

4 shorts

5 a tracksuit

6 a denim skirt

7 leggings

8 trousers

9 a headband

10 a necklace

Word Quest 2

1 cotton

2 wool

3 silk

4 denim

5 leather

Learning to LEARN Go to the Bilingual Dictionary (Activity Book, page 24).

51 words and expressions

Grammar Quest — Present continuous and Present simple

Affirmative and negative

Now		
I	**'m** wear**ing** / **'m not** wear**ing**	trousers.
He / She	**'s** help**ing** / **isn't** help**ing**	Sandra. / Cassy.
We / You / They	**'re** wear**ing** / **aren't** wear**ing**	leggings.

In general (always/often/sometimes/never)		
I / You	wear / **don't** wear	trousers.
He / She	help**s** / **doesn't** help	Sandra. / Cassy.
We / You / They	wear / **don't** wear	leggings.

Questions and short answers

Are	you	help**ing**	Dave**?**
Is	he/she		

Yes, I **am**.	Yes, he/she **is**.
No, I **'m not**.	No, he/she **isn't**.

Do	you	help	Dave**?**
Does	he/she		

Yes, I **do**.	Yes, he/she **does**.
No, I **don't**.	No, he/she **doesn't**.

Learning to LEARN Go to Unit 2 in your Grammar Builder.

19

Everyday English

1 **LISTENING** Listen and answer the questions.

1. Which picture is it – A or B?
2. Why is the boy buying a polo shirt?
3. What size is the polo shirt – small, medium or large?

2 SPEAKING Talk with a partner. How are pictures A and B different?

> In picture A, the boy is wearing a blue polo shirt.

> In picture B, the boy is wearing an orange polo shirt.

3 Listen, read and repeat. Act it out.

- Hello! Can I help you?
- Yes, please. I'd like to buy some shorts.
- Ok. What size would you like?
- I'm not sure. Small or medium, I think.
- Well, these shorts are small.
- **Can I try them on?**
- Yes. **The changing room is on the left.**
- Thank you.
- How are the shorts?
- They're great, thanks.

Marvellous Myths

Lesson 1

1 **Listen and repeat the words.**

1 brave

2 frightened

3 strong

4 weak

5 lucky

6 unlucky

7 difficult

8 easy

9 dangerous

10 safe

2 Quest Memory Game. Listen and play.

3 **Listen and read. Sing the song.**

It's the time of brave knights
And mythical creatures.
Strong men fight for their country and King.
A difficult time with dangerous adventures.
When the knights come home,
We hear the bells ring!

*It's the time of our
myths and legends.
The time of our magical past.
It's the time of our
myths and legends.
The magic goes by so fast.*

It's the time of wizards and magical places.
Lucky girls dance with the knights they love.
An easy time with love all around,
With stars shining down from above!

Chorus

21

3 Lesson 2

4 **Listen to the story. Read.**

Do you like legends? Here's a legend from a long time ago. It's about King Arthur!

The Legend of King Arthur

1 It's the 6th century. There are lots of different kings in England. The knights are fighting for their kings.

I'm fighting for King Uther. He's the most important king in England.

2 King Uther and his Queen have got a baby boy. His name is Arthur.

Our country is very dangerous. We need to hide Arthur in the safest place possible.

Merlin the wizard can help us.

3 Merlin takes the baby Arthur to a kind family in the countryside.

Please look after Arthur and don't tell anyone he's King Uther's baby. It's an important secret.

Of course. Our son's name is Kay. He can be Arthur's older brother.

4 15 years later, King Uther dies. Other kings and knights want to be the most important king in England.

I can be the most important king now.

No, I'm the bravest knight. I want to be the king.

5 In London, a mysterious sword appears in a stone.

The person who pulls out this sword is the real King of England.

I'm the strongest knight in England, but I can't pull out this sword!

6 Arthur is now 15 years old. One day, he goes to London with Kay.

Bring my sword, Arthur. Don't forget.

7 But Arthur forgets Kay's sword …

Oh no! I'm the unluckiest boy in London.

8 Then, Arthur sees the sword in the stone. He goes to the stone and pulls it out!

Oh good! I can give this sword to Kay.

That young man has got the sword. Amazing! What's his name?

It's Arthur! Arthur is the real King of England. Long live King Arthur!

9 And so the legend continues … Arthur becomes the King of England. He lives in Camelot, and Merlin the wizard helps him. King Arthur marries Princess Guinevere. He's a very strong king and his knights are the bravest knights in the country. They fight dragons and have lots of amazing adventures together. Do you know any more stories about the legend of King Arthur?

3 Lesson 3

5 Let's investigate grammar.

Revision – Comparative adjectives

I'm	unluck**ier**		you.
You're	strong**er**	**than**	me.
He's/She's	**more** important		them.

To be + superlative adjectives

I'm	**the** unluck**iest**	boy in London.
You're	**the** strong**est**	knight in England.
He's	**the most** important	king in England.
She's		queen in England.

6 Answer the questions. Look at the Grammar Quest to help you.

1. Do we add **the most** to **one-syllable adjectives** or **longer adjectives**?
2. Do we use **the** or **than** to make **superlative adjectives**?
3. With adjectives **ending in y**, do we add **-est** or **-iest**?

7 Listen, read and repeat. Act it out.

The legend of *The princess and the dragon*

Kiera: Today, Quest TV is doing a play about a famous legend.
Jack: I play the most important knight in the country.
Kiera: And I play the princess.
Jack: I'm the strongest knight!
Kiera: Yes, Jack! The play is about a very dangerous dragon. The knight wants to save the princess.
Jack: She's the luckiest princess in the country!
Kiera: But first the knight needs to fight the dragon. The knight is very frightened …
Jack: Because the dragon is very big and strong.
Kiera: But the knight forgets his sword.
Jack: Oh?
Kiera: So the princess kills the dragon and she's the bravest person in the country!

3 Lesson 4

8 Listen and repeat the words.

Word Quest 2

1 interesting   2 boring   3 clever   4 silly   5 magical

9 Listen and read. Answer the question.

Text type: a film review

How many adjectives from Activity 8 can you find in the review?

The Chronicles of Narnia
The Voyage of the Dawn Treader

★★★★½

This is my favourite film. The story is about the mythical land of Narnia. Lucy and Edmond go to Narnia through a magical painting. Their cousin Eustace goes with them. He's really silly. Lucy and Edmond meet Prince Caspian on a big boat called 'The Dawn Treader'. They travel to different islands and help him go to Aslan's country. There, they meet Aslan, the bravest lion in the world. I think the film is interesting because there are lots of amazing mythical creatures and clever special effects, too. My favourite character in the film is Reepicheep. He's a very clever mouse and he can talk. He's the funniest character in the film.

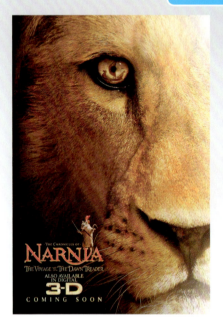

What's your favourite film?

10 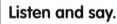 Listen and answer the questions you hear. Listen and check.

11  Listen and say.

Funky Phonics

This new film is interesting.
There's lots of dangerous action.
The hero is my favourite actor.
He's clever and attractive.

3 Lesson 5 CLIL Languages and Literature

12 Listen and read. Answer the audience questions.

Mythical creatures in Literature

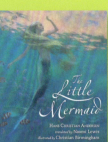

Audience Questions:
1. Which creatures are sometimes soldiers? SMS from Sally in England
2. Can a dragon fly? SMS from Andrew in Scotland
3. Who is the author of *The Little Mermaid*? SMS from Kathryn in Wales
4. Which creature is part horse? SMS from Patrick in Ireland

A centaur

A centaur is part man and part horse. It's got a man's head and torso, and it's got a horse's body and legs. It can talk like a man and it can run like a horse.

In *The Chronicles of Narnia* books by CS Lewis, centaurs are soldiers. They're very clever and brave creatures.

Do you know?
A centaur has got two stomachs, a man's stomach and a horse's stomach. It eats a lot of food!

A mermaid

A mermaid is part woman and part fish. It's got a woman's head and torso, and it's got a fish's tail. It can sing like a woman and it can swim like a fish. In the book *The Little Mermaid* by Hans Christian Andersen, the mermaid falls in love with a human and wants to become a human, too. She's an unlucky creature.

Do you know?
A mermaid can live for a very long time – about 300 years!

A dragon

A dragon is part dinosaur, part snake and part bat. It's got a dinosaur's body and legs, a snake's tail and a bat's wings. A dragon can fly and it can breathe out fire. In the book *The Hobbit* by JRR Tolkien, the dragon is called Smaug. It loves treasure and it's a very dangerous creature.

Do you know?
Merlin the wizard from the 'Legend of King Arthur' is a Dragonlord. This means he can speak to and control dragons!

13 Read and say 'True' or 'False'.

1. A centaur can't talk.
2. A dragon is part snake.
3. A centaur is a very weak creature.
4. In *The Little Mermaid*, the mermaid wants to become a fish.

 What type of mythical creature is Pegasus?

3 Lesson 6

Culture Quiz

14 Do the quiz. Listen and check.

1. The Loch Ness Monster is a mythical creature from … .
   a) Wales   b) Scotland   c) Ireland

2. In the famous legend, St George kills a … with his sword.
   a) dragon   b) mermaid   c) unicorn

3. Bigfoot is a mythical creature from … .
   a) Australia   b) England   c) North America

4. Leprechauns are mythical creatures from Ireland. They usually wear … clothes.
   a) red   b) green   c) blue

5. Merlin, Harry Potter and Gandalf are famous … .
   a) mermaids   b) centaurs   c) wizards

15 Listen and read.

Star Writer

Write to Quest TV.
Invent and describe a mythical creature.

Language fact
In English literature, many stories for children begin with 'Once upon a time …'.

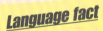

Email to: Quest TV

Dear Quest team,

My mythical creature is part shark and part eagle. It's got a shark's head and body, and it's got an eagle's legs and wings. It can swim like a shark and it can fly like an eagle. It's called a sharkeagle!

It isn't safe to be near a sharkeagle because it's the most dangerous creature in the world. It's very clever and it's the strongest creature in the world, too. All the other mythical creatures are frightened of my mythical creature!

Bye, Tony

Lesson 7:
Write your email (Activity Book, page 31).

Lesson 8:
Do the Progress Check (Activity Book, page 32).

Unit 3 Language Guide

Word Quest 1

 1 brave
 2 strong
 3 lucky
 4 difficult
 5 dangerous

 6 frightened
 7 weak
 8 unlucky
 9 easy
 10 safe

Word Quest 2

 1 interesting
 2 boring
 3 clever
 4 silly
 5 magical

Go to the Bilingual Dictionary (Activity Book, page 34). **53 words and expressions**

Grammar Quest

To be + superlative adjectives

I'm / You're	the unluck**iest**	boy in London.
He's / She's	**the most** important	king in England. / queen in England.
We're / You're / They're	the strong**est**	knights in England.

Remember!

brave → brav**er** → **the** brav**est**

easy → eas**ier** → **the** eas**iest**

frightened → **more** frightened → **the most** frightened

Go to Unit 3 in your Grammar Builder.

27

Everyday English

1 **LISTENING** Listen and answer the questions.

1 Which picture is it – A or B?
2 What type of books does the girl like?
3 What's Pam doing?

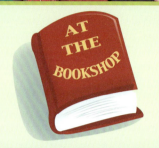

2 **SPEAKING** Talk with a partner. How are pictures A and B different?

> The female shop assistant in Picture A is weaker than the one in Picture B.

> The female shop assistant in Picture B is stronger than the one in Picture A.

3 Listen, read and repeat. Act it out.

- Excuse me?
- Yes. **How can I help you?**
- **I'm looking for** a book for my sister.
- Oh, that's a nice idea.
- Yes. It's her birthday.
- I see. What type of books does she like?
- She likes myths and legends.
- Well, we've got a new book. It's about a knight and a dragon.
- Great! That sounds interesting.
- Ok, I'll get it for you.

Let's Cook!

Lesson 1

1 **Listen and repeat the words.**

Word Quest 1

1 butter

2 milk

3 sugar

4 salt

5 a mango

6 a lemon

7 flour

8 a doughnut

9 a pancake

10 an omelette

2 **Quest Memory Game. Listen and play.**

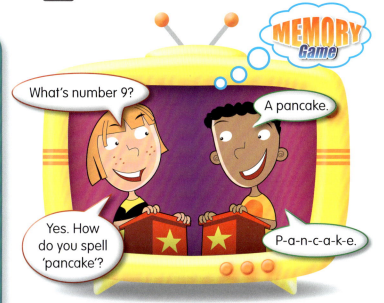

What's number 9?
A pancake.
Yes. How do you spell 'pancake'?
P-a-n-c-a-k-e.

3 **Listen and read. Sing the song.**

When I see you, I don't know what to say.
Your smile is so sweet.
It's like eating mangoes on a sunny day.

Your love is so sweet.
It's like sugar, sugar, yeah!
Your love is so sweet.
It's like sugar, sugar, yeah!

When you don't see me,
And you walk away.
There are tears in my eyes.
It's like eating lemons on a rainy day.

Chorus

When you talk to me, then I feel ok.
Your smile is so sweet.
It's like eating pancakes on a sunny day.

Chorus

4 Lesson 2

4 🎧 2/24 **Listen to the story. Read.**

Do you like watching cookery programmes on TV? Well, here's a story about a cookery programme. Let's see what happens!

1. Welcome to everyone's favourite cookery programme. It's *1, 2, 3, Let's Cook!* And here are our chefs. Hello, Monica and Nigel!

2. Ok! Here are your ingredients. There's some flour, there's some butter and there's some sugar. There are some lemons and there are some eggs, too. And remember chefs, you can't make the same food!

3. But you can each have one extra ingredient from our kitchen.

There aren't any mangoes in the bag. Are there any mangoes in the fridge?

Yes, there are.

4. There isn't any milk in the bag. Is there any milk in the fridge?

Yes, there is.

5. It's ten past four. You've got all your food and you've got twenty minutes. It's time … 1, 2, 3, let's cook!

6. 3, 2, 1! Let's stop! Now it's time for the chefs to tell us about their food.

This is my special mango cake. It's got flour, butter, eggs, sugar and mangoes.

And these are my special pancakes. They've got flour, butter, eggs, milk, sugar and lemons.

7. Your pancakes look great, Nigel. And your mango cake looks delicious, Monica!

Mmm! I'm hungry. Yuck! It's horrible!

This isn't sugar!

Yuck! It's salt!

8. Well, there's something very important to remember when you're cooking. Always check that it's sugar, not salt!

30

4 Lesson 3

5 Let's investigate grammar.

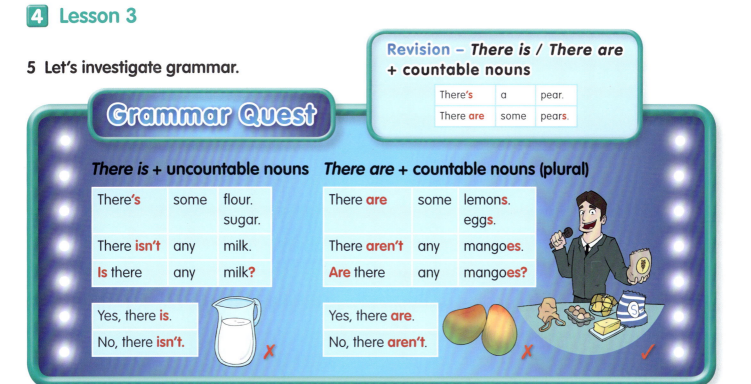

6 Answer the questions. Look at the Grammar Quest to help you.

1 Do we use **is some** or **are some** with **countable nouns**?
2 Do we use **There isn't** or **There aren't** with **uncountable nouns**?
3 Do we use **any** with **affirmative** or **negative sentences**?

7 Listen, read and repeat. Act it out.

Let's cook!

Sophie: I'm hungry.
Dan: Me too. Let's cook something.
Sophie: I can't cook. Can you cook, Dan?
Dan: Yes, I can. I can make pancakes. Are there any eggs?
Sophie: No, there aren't.
Dan: Oh! Is there any flour?
Sophie: No, there isn't. But there's some salt.
Dan: Oh dear! That's no good. I can't make pancakes now!
Sophie: I've got an idea! Let's go and buy some doughnuts!

8 Listen and repeat the words.

Word Quest 2

1 a cookery programme   2 a cartoon   3 a quiz show   4 a sports programme   5 a comedy series

9 Listen and read. Answer the question.

Text type: a class survey

How many children like watching cartoons more than other TV programmes?

Our favourite TV programmes

Hello! My name's Bianca and I go to Hillgate primary school in Manchester. Here are the results of my class survey about our favourite TV programmes. There are 25 children in my class.

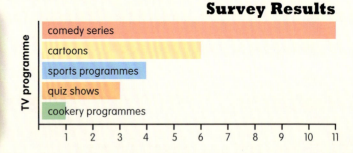

Survey Results

- 11 children like watching comedy series more than other TV programmes.
- 6 children like watching cartoons, especially *The Simpsons*.
- 4 children like watching sports programmes. Football and basketball are their favourite sports.
- 3 children like watching quiz shows, such as *Who wants to be a millionaire?*.
- Only 1 child likes watching cookery programmes.

Our favourite type of TV programme is a COMEDY SERIES!

What's your favourite type of TV programme?

10 Listen and answer the questions you hear. Listen and check.

11 Listen and say.

Cookery programmes are all about real food.
A comedy series is funny.
Cartoons contain lots of drawings,
And sports programmes have people running!

 **4** Lesson 5  **Social Science**

12 Listen and read. Answer the audience questions.

Food around the world

Audience Questions:

1 Which snack is popular in North Africa?
SMS from Paul in England

2 What are pancakes called in France?
SMS from Kenny in Scotland

3 Which snack is popular in South America?
SMS from Rhian in Wales

4 What do people in Germany often have in their pancakes?
SMS from Roisin in Ireland

Amazing fact
In the UK, people have pancake races on Pancake Day. They run and throw a pancake in the air!

Pancakes are popular in Europe, for example in France, Germany and the UK. People sometimes eat pancakes as a dessert or sometimes as a main meal. A pancake is often thin and flat. In the UK, people often eat pancakes on Pancake Day in February. In France, pancakes are called *crêpes*. In Germany, there are often potatoes in pancakes.

Amazing fact
The biggest alfajor biscuit in the world was made in Uruguay in 2010. It was 464 kg!

Baklava cakes are popular in North Africa, for example in Tunisia, Morocco and Egypt. People often eat *baklava* cakes as a dessert. A *baklava* cake is a small cake with nuts and honey. *Baklava* cakes are also popular in Turkey and Greece. In North Africa, there's a spice called cardamom in *baklava* cakes to give them a special taste.

Amazing fact
Honey is a main ingredient in a baklava cake. Honey bees have got five eyes!

 Alfajor biscuits are popular in South America, for example in Argentina, Uruguay and Peru. People often eat *alfajor* biscuits as a snack. An *alfajor* biscuit is two biscuits together with a layer of jam or *dulce de leche* in the middle. Traditionally, there's sugar on the top of an *alfajor* biscuit. Nowadays, there are lots of *alfajor* biscuits with chocolate on top, too.

13 Read and say 'True' or 'False'.

1 *Baklava* cakes are often thin and flat.
2 In Europe, people sometimes eat pancakes as a dessert or sometimes as a main meal.
3 A *crêpe* is another name for a *baklava* cake.
4 There are some *alfajor* biscuits with sugar on top.

 Which part of the world do *dan tat* cakes come from?

33

4 Lesson 6

Culture Quiz

14 Do the quiz. Listen and check.

1. People grow lots of ... in the UK.
   a) mangoes   b) oranges   c) apples

2. On Pancake Day in the UK, people traditionally put ... and sugar on their pancakes.
   a) lemon   b) salt   c) milk

3. A ... is another name for a biscuit in the USA.
   a) cake   b) doughnut   c) cookie

4. ... is the most popular hot drink in the UK.
   a) Milk   b) Tea   c) Coffee

5. Pancakes in the USA are ... pancakes in the UK.
   a) smaller than   b) bigger than   c) the same size as

15 Listen and read.

Write to Quest TV.
What's in your kitchen?

Language fact
In the UK, people often say 'It's a piece of cake!' if something is easy.

In the cupboard, there's some flour and there's some sugar. But there isn't any salt. In the fridge, there's some butter and there are some eggs. There aren't any lemons, but there are some oranges. I can make an orange cake!

By Rebecca

Lesson 7:
Write your description (Activity Book, page 41).

Lesson 8:
Do the Progress Check (Activity Book, page 42).

Unit 4 Language Guide

Word Quest 1

1 butter

2 sugar

3 a mango

4 flour

5 a pancake

6 milk

7 salt

8 a lemon

9 a doughnut

10 an omelette

Word Quest 2

1 a cookery programme

2 a cartoon

3 a quiz show

4 a sports programme

5 a comedy series

 Go to the Bilingual Dictionary (Activity Book, page 44).   **50 words and expressions**

Grammar Quest

There is + uncountable nouns
Affirmative and negative

There**'s**	some	flour. sugar.
There **isn't**	any	milk.

There are + countable nouns (plural)
Affirmative and negative

There **are**	some	lemon**s**. egg**s**.
There **aren't**	any	mango**es**.

Questions and short answers

Is there	any	milk**?**
Yes, there **is**.	No, there **isn't**.	

Questions and short answers

Are there	any	mango**es?**
Yes, there **are**.	No, there **aren't**.	

Remember!
some = affirmative
any = negative and questions

 Go to Unit 4 in your Grammar Builder.

Everyday English

1 **LISTENING**   Listen and answer the questions.

1. Which picture is it – A or B?
2. What's the surname of the actor on TV?
3. How old is the cat?

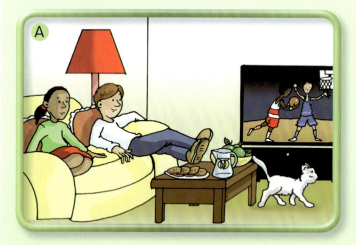

2 SPEAKING   Talk with a partner. How are pictures A and B different?

- In picture A, the cat is awake.
- In picture B, the cat is asleep.

3 Listen, read and repeat. Act it out.

- What are you doing?
- I'm watching TV.
- What are you watching?
- It's a cookery programme.
- **Can you change the channel?**
- **All right.** Look, there's a cartoon on this channel.
- Oh, I don't like cartoons. What else is on?
- There's a quiz show on this channel.
- Oh good. I like quiz shows.
- Ok. **Let's watch this.**

Quest TV 5 — Where Were You?

Lesson 1

1 Listen and repeat the words.

Word Quest 1

 1 a football stadium
 2 a shopping centre
 3 a police station
 4 a post office
 5 a palace
 6 a market
 7 a sports centre
 8 an airport
 9 a campsite
 10 an amusement park

2 Quest Memory Game. Listen and play.

What's number 4?

A post office.

That's right. Is there a post office where you live?

Yes, there is.

3 Listen and read. Sing the song.

Let me show you, this is London town.
Come with me, let's walk around!

Arrive at the airport, take the bus or the train.
Visit lots of places, never mind the rain.
Go to Buckingham Palace, stand by the gate.
See the guards on their horses.
They're really great!

Chorus

There's Camden market,
for lots of funky clothes.
There are shopping centres
everywhere you go.
There are football stadiums,
with people crowding in.
They want to see their football teams
win, win, win!

Chorus

5 Lesson 2

4 Listen to the story. Read.

5 Lesson 3

5 Let's investigate grammar.

6 Answer the questions. Look at the Grammar Quest to help you.

1. When we talk about the past, do we use **was** or **were** with **I** and **He/She**?
2. Do we use **was** or **were** with **We**?
3. Do we use **Were … ?** or **Was … ?** to ask a question with **He/She**?

7 Listen, read and repeat. Act it out.

5 Lesson 4

8 Listen and repeat the words.

1 last month   2 last weekend   3 last week   4 yesterday   5 last night

9 Listen and read. Answer the question.

Text type: **a blog**

Where was the lead singer yesterday?

Star Band Blog

home | about us | photos | fan club

Welcome to the Star Band blog! I'm Tom, the drummer.

Hi guys! We were happy on tour in the USA, but we're even happier now we're home!

June
25th New York
27th San Francisco
29th Los Angeles

July
7th Bristol
8th Manchester
14th Liverpool
15th London

Welcome back! Last month we were on tour in the USA. We played in New York, San Francisco and Los Angeles. It was lots of fun!

Last weekend we were back in the UK for more great concerts. We played in Bristol and Manchester. Our fantastic fans were there to cheer us on!

Last week was quiet. There weren't any concerts and we had time to visit our families and friends. It's always good to go home. I love seeing my little dog, Josie!

And yesterday Jan, our lead singer, was at her favourite place with Sam, our backing singer – the shopping centre! And do you know where Ron and I were? We were at the amusement park. It was really cool!

Then, last night we were all back on stage in our hometown of Liverpool.

See you soon!

Who's your favourite famous person?

10 Listen and answer the questions you hear. Listen and check.

11 Listen and say.

Funky Phonics

Last **m**onth, on a Sunday **n**ight,
To**m** and Ro**n** played the dru**m**s.

Last **n**ight, o**n** a **M**onday **n**ight,
Ja**n** and Sa**m** played the pia**n**o.

40

5 Lesson 5 CLIL Social Science

12 Listen and read. Answer the audience questions.

Mysteries in the UK

Audience Questions:
1 How old is Stonehenge? SMS from Lisa in England
2 Where is Loch Ness? SMS from Paddy in Ireland
3 Why is Loch Ness a mysterious place? SMS from Colin in Scotland
4 Where can you find crop circles? SMS from Catrin in Wales

Amazing fact
Originally, there were more than 60 stones in Stonehenge.

Stonehenge is an ancient stone monument. It's about 4000 years old and it's in the south of England. Stonehenge is a group of very big stones organised in two circles. Some of the stones are 13 metres tall and weigh more than 50 tonnes each. Some of the stones come from about 250 kilometres away. There are different theories about Stonehenge. Was it a religious temple? Was it an astronomical site? Or was it a cemetery?

Amazing fact
There are more crop circles in England than in other countries.

Loch Ness is a very big lake in Scotland. Some people think that the Loch Ness Monster lives in the lake! According to reports, the Loch Ness Monster has got a small head, a long neck and a long body. There are different theories about the Loch Ness Monster. Is it really a monster? Is it a type of dinosaur? Or is it people's imaginations?

Amazing fact
Lots of people call the Loch Ness Monster 'Nessie'!

Crop circles are patterns in fields. They appear mysteriously at night and people see the patterns in the morning.
In the past, crop circles were often simple patterns. Nowadays, they are often more complicated mathematical or astronomical patterns. There are different theories about crop circles. Do aliens make them? Do mini tornadoes make them? Or do artists make them?

13 Read and say 'True' or 'False'.

1 Some people say Stonehenge was a cemetery.
2 Loch Ness is a big mountain in Scotland.
3 Some people say the Loch Ness Monster is really a type of dinosaur.
4 Crop circles often appear in forests.

What is mysterious about the Nazca Desert in Peru?

5 Lesson 6

Culture Quiz

14 Do the quiz. Listen and check.

1 The football club with the biggest football stadium in the UK is ... .
   a) Arsenal   b) Liverpool   c) Manchester United

2 ... is the name of the clock tower that is a very famous tourist attraction in London.
   a) Camden Market   b) Big Ben   c) Buckingham Palace

3 Walt Disney World® is the biggest amusement park in ... .
   a) Australia   b) the USA   c) Canada

4 The Royal Mail is the name of the British ... company.
   a) post office   b) airport   c) police station

5 Shell Island in ... has got one of the biggest campsites in Europe.
   a) England   b) Ireland   c) Wales

Language fact

In the UK, we often say 'There's no place like home!' when we're happy to be at home.

15 Listen and read.

Write to Quest TV.
Where were you last week?
Send us a photo.

Email to: Quest TV

Dear Quest team,

Last week I was at school, but on Friday we visited London on a school trip. It was great! Last weekend was really good, too. On Saturday, I was with my mum and dad. We were at the shopping centre. In the afternoon, I was at the sports centre. I played basketball! On Sunday morning, I visited the market with my mum.
In the afternoon, I was at the football stadium with my dad and my brother. We love football!

Yesterday was Monday and I was at school again. Last night I was at home with my family.

Love Sarah

Lesson 7:
Write your email (Activity Book, page 51).

Lesson 8:
Do the Progress Check (Activity Book, page 52).

Unit 5 Language Guide

Word Quest 1

 1 a football stadium
 2 a shopping centre
 3 a police station
 4 a post office
 5 a palace
 6 a market
 7 a sports centre
 8 an airport
 9 a campsite
 10 an amusement park

Word Quest 2

 1 last month
 2 last weekend
 3 last week
 4 yesterday
 5 last night

 Go to the Bilingual Dictionary (Activity Book, page 54).   **49 words and expressions**

Grammar Quest — Past simple – *to be*

Affirmative

I	was	at the airport.
You	were	at the amusement park.
He/She	was	at the football stadium.
We / You / They	were	at the shopping centre.

Negative

I	wasn't	at the airport.
You	weren't	at the amusement park.
He/She	wasn't	at the football stadium.
We / You / They	weren't	at the shopping centre.

Questions and short answers

| Were | you | at the football stadium? |
| Was | he/she | |

Yes, I **was**.	No, I **wasn't**.
Yes, we **were**.	No, we **weren't**.
Yes, he/she **was**.	No, he/she **wasn't**.

 Go to Unit 5 in your Grammar Builder.

Everyday English

1 **LISTENING** Listen and answer the questions.

1 Which picture is it – A or B?
2 Who was Jilly with, her mum or her dad?
3 What was Jilly's dessert?

2 **SPEAKING** Talk with a partner. How are pictures A and B different?

In picture A, there's a car and a motorbike in the street.

In picture B, there are two cars in the street.

3 Listen, read and repeat. Act it out.

- Hello! **Are you ready to order?**
- Yes, please.
- What would you like for your **starter**?
- Tomato soup, please.
- And what would you like for your **main course**?
- A hamburger, please.
- With chips or salad?
- With chips, please.
- And what would you like for your **dessert**?
- Ice cream, please.
- Thanks. It won't be long.

  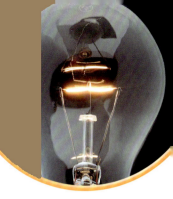

Eureka!

Lesson 1

1 Listen and repeat the words.

1 invent

2 discover

3 ask

4 answer

5 open

6 close

7 travel

8 return

9 start

10 finish

2 Quest Memory Game. Listen and play.

3 Listen and read. Sing the song.

What an interesting world we live in,
With so many places to see.
Open your eyes and look around you,
What an incredible place to be!

What an interesting world we live in,
With so many things to do.
Always remember to ask lots of questions.
Think a lot – discover something new!

Don't close your eyes,
Keep them wide open.
Travel the world
and meet different people.
Always remember to ask
aots of questions.
Start today – discover something new!
Start today – discover something new!

Repeat chorus

6 Lesson 2

4 **Listen to the story. Read.**

Lesson 3

5 Let's investigate grammar.

Revision – Present simple and Past simple

| I | play | tennis. | I | played | tennis. |
| He/She | plays | | He/She | | |

Grammar Quest

Past simple – regular verbs

| I He/She They | ask**ed** **didn't** ask | for a special dessert. |
| | invent**ed** **didn't** invent | the ice cream cone. |

| **Did** | you he/she they | invent | a new flavour**?** | Yes, I/he/she/they **did**. No, I/he/she/they **didn't**. |

6 Answer the questions. Look at the Grammar Quest to help you.

1. Do we add **-ed** to the verb in **affirmative** or **negative** sentences?
2. Do we put **didn't** before the verb in **affirmative** or **negative** sentences?
3. In **questions**, do we add **-ed** to the verb or put **Did** before the verb?

7 🎧 Listen, read and repeat. Act it out.

Our favourite inventors and inventions

Jack: My favourite scientist is Albert Einstein.
Sophie: Did he invent something important?
Jack: Yes, he did. He discovered important scientific theories.
Sophie: Wow! Well, do you know who invented Converse shoes?
Jack: No, who was it?
Sophie: It was a man called Mr Converse! He invented them for basketball players.
Jack: That's interesting. And do you know that they produced the first MP3 player in 1999?
Sophie: Really? What other famous inventions do you know about?
Jack: A boy called Philo Farnsworth invented the first electronic TV when he was only 15 years old.
Sophie: That's amazing!

6 Lesson 4

8 Listen and repeat the words.

Word Quest 2

1 First, …   2 Then, …   3 After that, …   4 Later, …   5 Finally, …

9 Listen and read. Answer the question.

Text type: a biography

What did the doctor finally discover?

Edward Jenner

A doctor
Edward Jenner was born in England in 1749. First, he was at school. Then, he helped a doctor in his village. After that, he travelled to London and he studied with another doctor in a hospital. Finally, he returned to his village as a doctor himself.

A scientist
At this time, there was a horrible disease called smallpox. There was also a disease called cowpox. Smallpox was more dangerous than cowpox. It killed lots of people, especially children. Edward Jenner wanted to help people with smallpox, so he experimented with these diseases.

His discovery
He discovered that cowpox was a vaccination for smallpox. This was a very important discovery. It helped millions of people all over the world.

Jenner's famous experiment
There was a cow called Blossom, a milkmaid called Sarah and a boy called James. Sarah had cowpox. First, Jenner infected James with the cowpox from Sarah. Then, he infected James with smallpox. The cowpox stopped the smallpox.

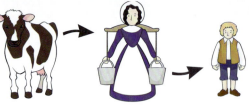

Do you know?
The word *vaccination* comes from the Latin word *vacca*, because of Jenner's experiment with Blossom the cow.

What was your last vaccination for?

10 Listen and answer the questions you hear. Listen and check.

11 Listen and say.

Funky Phonics

Doctor To**dd** **d**i**d**n't know what he want**ed** to **d**o.
First, he want**ed** to write a car**d**.
Later, he want**ed** to ri**d**e in a cart.
Doctor To**dd** **d**i**d**n't know what he want**ed** to **d**o!

 Lesson 5  Science

12 Listen and read. Answer the audience questions.

Young inventors

Let's find out who invented these things.

Audience Questions:

1 Who invented ear muffs?
SMS from David in England

2 Why did Katherine Gregory invent Wristies®?
SMS from Mary in Scotland

3 What are Little Bundies?
SMS from Aled in Wales

4 Which inventor opened a factory?
SMS from Colleen in Ireland

Chester Greenwood invented **ear muffs**. He was only 15 years old! He was born in the USA in 1858. He liked ice skating but he didn't like his ears getting cold, so he invented ear muffs. Then, he opened Greenwood's Ear Protector Factory. Nowadays, lots of people wear ear muffs.

Amazing fact
Chester's grandma helped him make his first ear muffs. She sewed them!

Katherine Gregory invented **Wristies®**. She was only 10 years old! She was born in the USA in 1984. She liked playing in the snow but she didn't like her wrists getting cold, so she invented Wristies® to go under her gloves and coat. Later, she opened the Wristies® company. Now, lots of people wear Wristies®.

Amazing fact
Luisa's favourite Little Bundy doll is called Olivia. She says Olivia looks like her cousin!

Amazing fact
Now, there are also heated Wristies®. They've got pockets in them for a battery-operated heater!

Luisa Bundy invented **Little Bundies**. She was only 12 years old! She was born in the UK in 1995. She liked making little dolls for her friends. Her friends loved her dolls, so she invented a group of little dolls called Little Bundies. Later, she patented her dolls. Today, lots of children buy Luisa's dolls from different shops.

13 Read and say 'True' or 'False'.

1 Chester was from Australia.
2 Chester invented ear muffs because he liked ice skating.
3 Katherine invented Wristies® because her feet were cold.
4 Luisa liked making little dolls for her friends.

 What did Blaise Pascal invent when he was a teenager?

Lesson 6

Culture Quiz

14 Do the quiz. Listen and check.

1. A man called … invented denim jeans . He lived in the USA.
   a) Leo Strand   b) Levi Strauss   c) Lenny Smith
2. Sir Alexander Fleming was from Scotland. He discovered an important … called penicillin.
   a) animal   b) food   c) medicine
3. A woman called Mary Anderson from … invented windscreen wipers for cars in 1903.
   a) the USA   b) the UK   c) New Zealand
4. The British explorer Captain James Cook discovered … when he travelled around the world in 1770.
   a) Canada   b) Australia   c) China
5. Dr John Pemberton from the USA invented a famous drink called … .
   a) lemonade   b) coffee   c) Coca-Cola®

Language fact
In the UK, you can say 'That sounds like a great idea!' if you think someone has got a very good idea.

15 Listen and read.

Write to Quest TV.
Write a biography of a famous inventor or discoverer.

A biography of Mark Zuckerberg, the co-inventor of Facebook
Facebook is a website for people over 13 years old. People can communicate with friends and family. Mark Zuckerberg invented Facebook with a friend. He was born in the USA in 1984. He started programming computers when he was a child. Then, he travelled to Harvard University where he studied Computer Science. Later, he developed the famous website. Finally, Facebook opened to the public in 2006. There are about 800 million people who use Facebook!
By Carl

Lesson 7:
Write your biography (Activity Book, page 61).

Lesson 8:
Do the Progress Check (Activity Book, page 62).

Unit 6 Language Guide

Word Quest 1

1 invent   2 ask   3 open   4 travel   5 start

6 discover   7 answer   8 close   9 return   10 finish

Word Quest 2

1 First, …   2 Then, …   3 After that, …   4 Later, …   5 Finally, …

 Go to the Bilingual Dictionary (Activity Book, page 64).   **51 words and expressions**

Grammar Quest — Past simple – regular verbs

Affirmative and negative

I You He She We You They	ask**ed** **didn't** ask	for a special dessert.
	invent**ed** **didn't** invent	the ice cream cone.
	visit**ed** **didn't** visit	the museum.

Questions and short answers

Did	you he she we you they	invent	a new flavour**?**

Yes,	I you he she we you they	**did**.
No,		**didn't**.

 Go to Unit 6 in your Grammar Builder.

Remember!
travel → travel**led**
study → stud**ied**

Everyday English

1 **LISTENING** Listen and answer the questions.

1 Which picture is it – A or B?
2 Who's giving a vaccination?
3 What's the old medical book about?

2 **SPEAKING** Talk with a partner. How are pictures A and B different?

"In picture A, the girl has got curly brown hair."

"In picture B, the girl has got straight brown hair."

3 Listen, read and repeat. Act it out.

- Hello, James. How are you feeling?
- Not so good.
- **What's the matter?**
- **My leg hurts.**
- What happened?
- I was in a football match.
- Oh! You need some cream. Here's a prescription.
- Thank you, doctor.
- Take care, James.
- Thanks. Bye.

On Safari

Lesson 1

1 Listen and repeat the words.

Word Quest 1

Yesterday, …

1. I **went** on safari.
2. I **went** to bed.
3. I **said** hello.
4. I **said** goodbye.
5. I **ate** a sandwich.
6. I **ate** a pineapple.
7. I **saw** zebras.
8. I **saw** lions.
9. I **wrote** emails.
10. I **wrote** postcards.

2 Quest Memory Game. Listen and play.

What's number 5?
I ate a sandwich.
That's right! What's the present simple of 'ate'?
Eat.

3 Listen and read. Sing the song.

So what did we see, on safari?
We saw zebras in the grass.
We went on safari, on safari.
And saw zebras in the grass!

We say wanyama*, wanyama!
We say wanyama, wanyama!

So what did we see, on safari?
We saw leopards in the trees.
We went on safari, on safari.
We saw leopards in the trees.

Chorus

So what did we see, on safari?
We saw lions by the lake.
We went on safari, on safari.
We saw lions by the lake.

Chorus

*wanyama means animals in Swahili

7 Lesson 2

4 Listen to the story. Read.

Why is Jane Goodall, an anthropologist from the UK, famous? Let's find out!

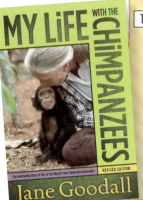

1 Jane Goodall studied chimpanzees and wrote lots of books about them. She received many awards for her work. Thanks to Jane Goodall, we know more about chimpanzees and how similar they are to people.

2 Jane was always interested in animals. When she was only four years old, she watched a group of hens for hours to see how they lay eggs.

3 Her favourite books were *Doctor Doolittle* and *Tarzan*.

Doctor Doolittle helps animals. One day, I want to help animals, too.

4 When Jane was 23 years old, she went to Africa. She met Louis Leakey, an important anthropologist.

Jane, we need someone to go to the Gombe Reserve to study the chimpanzees.

I'd like to go, please.

5 So, in 1960, Jane went to the Gombe Reserve. At first, Jane didn't see many chimpanzees. They were shy.

Oh no! I can't see the chimpanzees very well.

6 But Jane didn't stop. She waited and waited. Finally, she saw the chimpanzees. She watched and learnt lots of new things about them.

Wow! That chimpanzee is eating meat. Chimpanzees aren't vegetarians!

Amazing! That chimpanzee is using a grass stem as a tool to get the ants. People aren't the only ones who can use tools.

Look! Chimpanzees live together in groups and they look after each other. They're similar to us!

7 Later, Jane wrote about the chimpanzees in her notebook.

Today, I watched the chimpanzees in their natural environment and this is what I saw. They ate meat. They used grass stems as tools. They lived in groups and looked after each other. Chimpanzees are similar to people in lots of ways. They're clever animals and we need to protect them.*

8 Jane loved chimpanzees. She started many organisations and conservation projects to protect animals and the natural world.

* This text is an example of what Jane Goodall may have written.

54

7 Lesson 3

5 Let's investigate grammar.

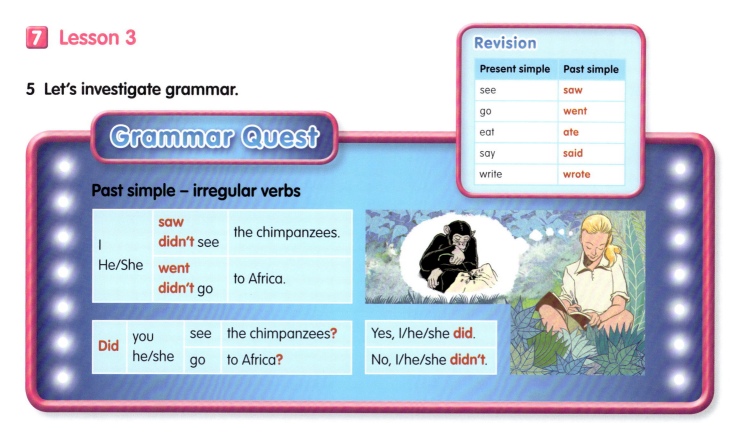

6 Answer the questions. Look at the Grammar Quest to help you.

1. Do we **change the verb** or **add -ed to the verb** in **affirmative** sentences?
2. Do we put **didn't** before the verb in **affirmative** or **negative** sentences?
3. In **short answers**, do we use **the verb** or **did**/**didn't**?

7 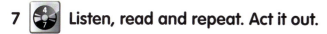 Listen, read and repeat. Act it out.

On safari

Dan: Last year, I went on safari in Kenya with my family.
Kiera: Did you see lots of amazing animals?
Dan: Yes, I did! But one day, something terrible happened!
Kiera: Oh no! What happened?
Dan: Well, we saw a lion and it walked towards our car.
Kiera: Oh dear! Then what happened?
Dan: I said, 'Don't move!' The lion looked at us and …
Kiera: What? What did the lion do?
Dan: It was hungry, so it ate my brother's …
Kiera: Oh no!
Dan: … sandwich!
Kiera: Oh Dan!

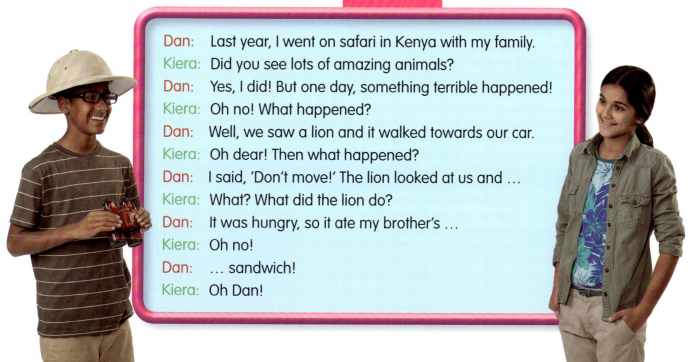

7 Lesson 4

8 Listen and repeat the words.

Word Quest 2

1 a buffalo   2 an ostrich   3 an antelope   4 a leopard   5 a vulture

9 Listen and read. Answer the question.

Text type: a fact file

Which two animals in Activity 8 are NOT in the fact file?

Animals of Africa

Common ostrich

Adult size:	about 2.7 metres tall
Adult weight:	about 130 kilos
Food:	omnivore (mainly plants and some insects)
Habitat:	mainly the savannahs and deserts in Africa
Special ability:	It uses its wings to balance when it runs.

Do you know? An ostrich can kill a person with its legs!

African leopard

Adult size:	about 1.5 metres tall
Adult weight:	between 50 kilos and 80 kilos
Food:	carnivore (big and small animals)
Habitat:	the jungles, savannahs and deserts in Africa
Special ability:	It can climb trees and it can swim.

Do you know? A leopard can see in the dark and it hunts at night!

White-backed vulture

Adult size:	about 1 metre tall
Adult weight:	between 5 kilos and 7 kilos
Food:	carnivore (dead animals)
Habitat:	mainly the savannahs in Africa
Special ability:	It can soar (fly without moving its wings) for hours.

Do you know? A vulture hasn't got feathers on its head and neck!

What's your favourite African animal?

10 Listen and answer the questions you hear. Listen and check.

11 Listen and say.

Funky Phonics

Ele**ph**ants can't speak **F**rench.
Frogs aren't very good at Geogra**ph**y.
Bu**ff**aloes don't study **Ph**ysics.
Because animals are di**ff**erent
From you and me!

7 Lesson 5 CLIL Natural Science

12 Listen and read. Answer the audience questions.

There are lots of different types of animals and plants that live on our planet. This is called *biodiversity*. Lots of animals and plants are in danger of extinction. Animals and plants need a habitat to live in. People are destroying lots of these habitats. Animal conservation helps protect animals, especially endangered animals and their natural habitats.

Audience Questions:
1 What does biodiversity mean?
SMS from Alison in England
2 Do animals live in cages in a safari park?
SMS from Jim in Scotland
3 What's the main aim of an animal reserve?
SMS from Ellen in Wales
4 Can zoos help animal conservation?
SMS from Michael in Ireland

Endangered animal fact
Giant pandas are endangered animals from China. Panda reserves help protect them.

ANIMAL CONSERVATION

Endangered animal fact
Golden lion tamarins are endangered animals from Brazil. Some zoos help re-introduce them into their natural habitat.

Zoos
Animals in a zoo live in cages or small enclosures. The main aim of a zoo is for people to see different animals from around the world.

Safari parks
A safari park is bigger than a zoo, and the animals don't live in cages. But there's a fence around the park. The main aim of a safari park is for people to see animals in a more natural environment.

Animal reserves
An animal reserve is a safe area of land where animals can live. There aren't any cages or fences. The main aim of an animal reserve is to protect animals.

Conservation work
Lots of zoos, safari parks and animal reserves help animal conservation:
- They can provide a safe place for animals to live.
- They can help endangered animals reproduce, and then help re-introduce them into their natural habitats.
- They can give money to conservation projects.

Endangered animal fact
One-horned rhinos from Nepal are endangered animals. Some safari parks provide a safe place for them to live.

13 Read and say 'True' or 'False'.

1 Animal conservation helps protect people.
2 The main aim of a zoo is for people to see animals.
3 A safari park has got a fence around it.
4 Animal reserves don't help animal conservation.

Find out about an endangered animal in your country.

7 Lesson 6

Culture Quiz

14 Do the quiz. Listen and check.

1. There are two types of elephants: African and ... elephants.
   a) American   b) Asian   c) British
2. London Zoo has got a conservation project to protect antelopes in the Sahara ... in Africa.
   a) desert   b) jungle   c) savannah
3. Yellowstone National Park is ... in the USA which protects many endangered animals, including the American buffalo.
   a) a safari park   b) a zoo   c) an animal reserve
4. Brown bears are now extinct in ... , but they lived there more than 1000 years ago.
   a) the UK   b) Africa   c) Canada
5. There are only about 40 Amur leopards left in their natural habitat in Russia. It's one of the most ... animals in the world.
   a) popular   b) protected   c) endangered

Language fact
In the UK, we say 'You've got a memory like an elephant!' if someone has got a very good memory.

15 Listen and read.

Write to Quest TV.
Imagine you went on a safari holiday. Send us a postcard about it!

Dear Quest team,
Last month I went on a safari holiday with my family. We travelled in a special safari car and we saw lots of animals. We saw elephants, buffaloes, antelopes, cheetahs, zebras and leopards. We didn't see an ostrich. My favourite African animal is a leopard. In the evening, we returned to our campsite and we ate hamburgers and chips. After that, we wrote lots of postcards. It was an amazing holiday!
Bye, Max

Quest team
Quest TV
P.O. Box 67
London
the UK

Lesson 7:
Write your postcard (Activity Book, page 71).

Lesson 8:
Do the Progress Check (Activity Book, page 72).

Unit 7 Language Guide

Word Quest 1

1 I **went** on safari.

3 I **said** hello.

3 I **ate** a sandwich.

4 I **saw** zebras.

5 I **wrote** emails.

6 I **went** to bed.

7 I **said** goodbye.

8 I **ate** a pineapple.

9 I **saw** lions.

10 I **wrote** postcards.

Word Quest 2

1 a buffalo

2 an ostrich

3 an antelope

4 a leopard

5 a vulture

Go to the Bilingual Dictionary (Activity Book, page 74). **52 words and expressions**

Grammar Quest — Past simple – irregular verbs

Affirmative and negative

I You He She We You They	**saw** **didn't** see	the chimpanzees.
	went **didn't** go	to Africa.
	wrote **didn't** write	in a notebook.

Questions and short answers

	you he she we you they	see	the chimpanzees?
Did		go	to Africa?

Yes,	I you he she we you they	**did**.
No,		**didn't**.

Go to Unit 7 in your Grammar Builder.

Everyday English

1 **LISTENING** Listen and answer the questions.

1. Which picture is it – A or B?
2. Where did Abby go on a safari holiday?
3. Who did Abby go with?

2 **SPEAKING** Talk with a partner. How are pictures A and B different?

- In picture A, there's a lion in the grass.
- In picture B, there's a lion behind the tree.

3 Listen, read and repeat. Act it out.

- I'm so excited. We're in a safari park!
- Look! There's a zebra.
- I can't see it. **Where is it?**
- **It's over there.**
- Oh yes! It's eating grass.
- And look! There are some white rhinos.
- I can't see them. **Where are they?**
- **They're over there.**
- Oh yes! They're very big.
- Ok, now let's find some leopards.
- Cool!

  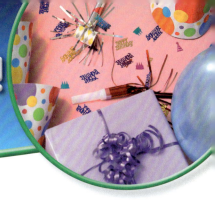

Party Time!

Lesson 1

1 Listen and repeat the words.

Word Quest 1

1 a party

2 an invitation

3 snacks

4 fizzy drinks

5 paper plates

6 paper cups

7 a band

8 speakers

9 balloons

10 streamers

2 Quest Memory Game. Listen and play.

3 Listen and read. Sing the song.

*Let's have a party, come on everyone!
It's time for a party, it's time for some fun!*

Let's have a party, come on everyone!
Send invitations to friends
near and far.
It doesn't matter who they are.
Let's have a party,
It's time for some fun!

Let's have a party,
Come on everyone!
Balloons and streamers everywhere.
Fizzy drinks and snacks for us to share.
Let's have a party, it's time for some fun!

Let's have a party, come on everyone!
All of us dancing the night away.
Enjoy the music that our band can play.
Let's have a party, it's time for some fun!

Chorus

8 Lesson 3

5 Let's investigate grammar.

6 Answer the questions. Look at the Grammar Quest to help you.

1 Do we use **going** or **going to** in this form of the **future** tense?
2 Do we use **isn't going to** with **I** or **he/she** in **negative** sentences?
3 Do we use **going to** in the **short answers**?

7 Listen, read and repeat. Act it out.

 **Lesson 4**

8 Listen and repeat the words.

Word Quest 2

1 make friends   2 get a job   3 get married   4 have children   5 go on holiday

9 Listen and read. Answer the question.

Text type: a horoscope

Which *future numbers* include going on holiday?

Find out about your future!

Do you want to know about your future? All you need is your *future number*!

a	e	i	o	u
1	2	3	4	5

Here's how you do it:

- Write down your first name and surname.

  Elizabeth Smith

- Add the numbers for the vowels in your name.

  2 + 3 + 1 + 2 + 3 = 11

- If your final number is 10 or more, add the numbers again to get a single number.

  1 + 1 = 2 ← This is your *future number*!

- Find your *future number* in the horoscope and read about your future!

Horoscope

1 You're going to be a pop singer. You're going to have five children.

2 You're going to get a job with animals. You're going to go on a safari holiday.

3 You aren't going to be an artist. You're going to make lots of friends.

4 You aren't going to be a teacher. You're going to be very happy.

5 You're going to get a job in TV. You're going to have lots of money.

6 You're going to get married. You aren't going to be rich.

7 You're going to go on lots of holidays. You aren't going to be famous.

8 You're going to be a doctor. You're going to have two children.

9 You're going to be a sports star. You're going to have a long life.

Are you happy with your *future number*?

10 Listen and answer the questions you hear. Listen and check.

11 Listen and say.

Jennifer and **J**onathan are going to get **j**obs as **j**ournalists in the **j**ungle.

Harry and **H**elen are going to **h**ave a **h**appy **h**oliday in **H**olland.

8 Lesson 5 CLIL History

12 Listen and read. Answer the audience questions.

The History of Birthday Celebrations

Hi! I'm Tina and I'm from the UK. It's my birthday on Saturday and I'm going to have a party with my friends. I'm going to have a birthday cake with candles on it, and everyone is going to sing *Happy Birthday* to me! But where do these birthday traditions come from?

Audience Questions:

1 Which country had the first birthday parties for children?
SMS from Joe in Scotland

2 Who did the Ancient Greeks give cakes to?
SMS from Sian in Wales

3 What shape were Ancient Greek cakes?
SMS from Simon in England

4 Why do people give birthday cards in the UK?
SMS from Erin in Ireland

Amazing fact
In some parts of Canada, it's traditional to put butter on a child's nose on his or her birthday.

Why do we have birthday parties?
More than 2000 years ago, many people believed that bad spirits visited a person on his or her birthday. So friends visited people on their birthdays to stop these bad spirits. At first, only very important people, like kings, celebrated their birthdays with a real party. In Europe, the first birthday parties for children were probably in Germany. They were called *kinderfeste*.

Amazing fact
In some countries, like Spain and Brazil, it's traditional to pull a child's ear on his or her birthday!

Where do birthday cakes come from?
The Ancient Greeks made cakes for Artemis, the Goddess of the Moon. The cakes were round and they had candles on them. The cakes looked like the moon. Nowadays, people make or buy birthday cakes in different shapes and sizes.

13 Read and say 'True' or 'False'.

1 In the past, people believed bad spirits visited them on their birthday.
2 Kings celebrated their birthdays with *kinderfeste* parties.
3 The Ancient Greeks put candles on their cakes.
4 People in the UK never give birthday cards.

Where do birthday cards come from?
In the UK, the tradition of birthday cards started more than 100 years ago. People in the UK always give birthday cards to say *Happy Birthday* to their family and friends. Nowadays, some people send e-cards on the computer, too.

Online Quest Which country does the famous *Happy Birthday* song come from?

8 Lesson 6

Culture Quiz

14 Do the quiz. Listen and check.

1 The UK celebrates the Queen's official birthday in ... every year.
   a) June   b) March   c) October
2 A ceilidh (we say 'kaylee') is a traditional Scottish ... .
   a) song   b) Food   c) party
3 In the UK, people traditionally give someone they love ... for Valentine's Day.
   a) a balloon   b) a card   c) a cake
4 In the USA, families often celebrate a girl's ... birthday with a special party.
   b) 20th   b) 10th   c) 16th
5 People in the UK often have a street party to celebrate a ... .
   a) royal wedding b) birthday   c) christening

Language fact
In the UK, we call a person who loves parties a 'party animal'!

Interesting fact
One of the biggest parties in the world is the carnival in Rio de Janeiro, Brazil, in February every year!

15 Listen and read.

Write to Quest TV.
You're going to have a party! Send us your party plans and your e-invitation.

Email to: Quest TV

Dear Quest team,

We're going to have a party to celebrate the end of the school year! Here's our party plan:
- I'm going to bring some snacks and paper plates.
- Paula is going to bring some fizzy drinks.
- Mark is going to bring some paper cups.
- Alex is going to bring some balloons.
- We aren't going to have a live band, Sally is going to bring her MP3 player and speakers for the music.

We're going to eat, dance and have lots of fun!

From Jenny

Invitation
You're invited to an
END-OF-YEAR PARTY!

Where: Lakeside school
When: Friday 28th June, 6pm

Please answer this e-invitation as soon as possible.

I'm going to come to the party:

Yes / No

Lesson 7:
Write your email and your e-invitation (Activity Book, page 81).

Lesson 8:
Do the Progress Check (Activity Book, page 82).

Unit 8 Language Guide

Word Quest 1

 1 a party
 2 snacks
 3 paper plates
 4 a band
 5 balloons

 6 an invitation
 7 fizzy drinks
 8 paper cups
 9 speakers
 10 streamers

Word Quest 2

 1 make friends
 2 get a job
 3 get married
 4 have children
 5 go on holiday

 Go to the Bilingual Dictionary (Activity Book, page 84).

46 words and expressions

Grammar Quest

Future – *to be* + *going to*, affirmative

I'm		buy balloons.
You're		buy streamers.
He's / She's	going to	bring speakers.
We're / You're / They're		dance.

Future – *to be* + *going to*, negative

I'm not		buy balloons.
You aren't		buy streamers.
He isn't / She isn't	going to	bring speakers.
We aren't / You aren't / They aren't		dance.

Future – *to be* + *going to*, questions and short answers

Are	you	going to	dance?
Is	he/she		
Are	we/you/they		

| Yes, I am. | Yes, he/she is. | Yes, we/you/they are. |
| No, I'm not. | No, he/she isn't. | No, we/you/they aren't. |

 Go to Unit 8 in your Grammar Builder.

Everyday English

1 **LISTENING** Listen and answer the questions.

1 Which picture is it – A or B?
2 When is Clare's birthday?
3 What's the name of the song?

2 **SPEAKING** Talk with a partner. How are pictures A and B different?

- In picture A, there are five balloons.
- In picture B, there are six balloons.

3 Listen, read and repeat. Act it out.

- Hi, Anna! It's James.
- Oh, hello James.
- I'm going to have a party this weekend. **Would you like to come?**
- **I'd love to!** Thanks.
- Great! It's on Saturday night, at my house.
- What can I bring?
- Nothing. It's all organised.
- Ok, then.
- So, see you on Saturday night at half past six.
- Yes. I can't wait!

New Year's Eve

1 Listen as you read. Answer the questions. Match the words to the pictures.

1 What do people say to each other at New Year?
2 What is *Auld Lang Syne*?

What do you do on New Year's Eve?

In London
My parents always have a party in our house on 31st December, New Year's Eve. We invite lots of friends. At **midnight**, we watch the TV and listen to **Big Ben** chime twelve times. Then, we all say *Happy New Year* and kiss each other. There are **fireworks** in the centre of London – they're great to watch!

Lily in London

In Edinburgh
New Year's Eve is my favourite night of the year. My family and I walk through the streets, and we carry special **torches**. Then, at midnight, **pipers** play the **bagpipes** to welcome in the New Year. They wear **kilts**. We all hold hands and sing a famous song called *Auld Lang Syne*. There's a bonfire and there are fireworks. It's a fantastic night!

Peter in Edinburgh

In New York
New Year's Eve in New York is very special. Thousands of people go to **Times Square**. There are lots of events, like musical performances and fireworks. And at midnight, **confetti** falls down from the buildings and onto the people standing in the square. It's all very beautiful to see!

Courtney in New York

How is your New Year's Eve similar or different?

2 Listen and read.

Hi, I'm Amber! On New Year's Day, my family and I make **New Year's Resolutions**. These are things that we want to do during the year ahead. Here are our resolutions for this year!

Our New Year's Resolutions

Me: I want to improve my Spanish!
Dad: I want to go to the gym and be more healthy.
Mum: I want to learn more about computers.
Sister: I want to play the drums!
Brother: I want to help my grandma more.

St Patrick's Day

1 Listen as you read. Answer the questions. Match the words to the pictures.

1 What date is St Patrick's Day?
2 What is a leprechaun?

Do you know about St Patrick's Day?

A celebration
I love St Patrick's Day. It's a special day in Ireland, and for Irish people all over the world. My cousins in New York celebrate, too. It's on 17th March, and it's a public holiday in Ireland. It's a celebration of St Patrick, and a celebration of our country and its culture. But mostly, it's a day of fun!

Calum in Cork

Dressing up
On St Patrick's Day, my family and I wear green clothes and we watch the **parade** together. My dad wears a silly green hat! I've got an **Irish flag**. It's green, orange and white. My little sister paints her hair green. We wear a **shamrock** on our jackets. We eat Irish food, listen to Irish music and do Irish dancing.

Sarah in Dublin

An Irish myth
Leprechauns are an important part of Irish culture. According to Irish myth, a **leprechaun** is a little old man. He mends shoes for Irish **fairies**. The fairies give the leprechaun gold as a thank you. And so the myth says it's good luck if you catch a leprechaun because you can have his **pot of gold**!

Paddy in Limerick

a   b   c   d

What special day do you celebrate in your country?

2 Listen and read.   **A St Patrick's Day poem**

St Patrick's Day is a day of fun.
In the rain or in the sun.
Green is the colour you must wear,
On your jacket, or in your hair.
It's a day of good luck for everyone!

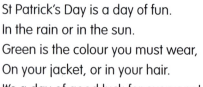

Do you know?
- Ireland is often called *The Emerald Isle* because it's a very green country.
- According to Irish myths, leprechauns wear green jackets.
- The shamrock is a symbol of St Patrick's Day and of Ireland.
- If you find a shamrock with four green leaves, it's good luck!
- A limerick is a funny poem often associated with Ireland.

Notting Hill Carnival

1 Listen as you read. Answer the questions. Match the words to the pictures.

1 When is the Notting Hill Carnival?
2 What type of celebration is the carnival, traditionally?

Do you know about the Notting Hill Carnival?

A celebration
My favourite celebration in London is the Notting Hill Carnival. It's on the last Sunday and Monday of August every year. Traditionally, it's a Caribbean celebration. Nowadays, people from lots of different countries and cultures come together to celebrate. **Anna in South London**

Parades
I like watching the Notting Hill Carnival parades. On Sunday, there's the **children's parade**. The children look great in their costumes. On Monday, there's the main parade. There are lots of floats and people wear **bright costumes**. Everyone looks amazing! **Silvia in Brighton**

Music
I love the music at the Notting Hill Carnival. There are fantastic **steel bands** playing Caribbean music. There are also other bands playing different kinds of music, like reggae, hip hop and jazz. I love dancing to the music! **Justin in Birmingham**

Food
I like the food at the Notting Hill Carnival. There are lots of **food stalls** which sell a variety of food. You can eat food from different countries around the world. My favourite food at the carnival is **sweetcorn**. But all the food is delicious! **Reggie in East London**

Is there a big carnival celebration in your country?

2 Listen and read. Sing the song.

Come to the Notting Hill Carnival.
Come and celebrate with everyone.
Come to the Notting Hill Carnival.
Come and have some fun!

People are wearing amazing costumes,
And walking down the street.
People are dancing to fantastic music,
Smiling at the people they meet.

Chorus

Macmillan Education
Between Towns Road, Oxford OX4 3PP
A division of Macmillan Publishers Limited

Companies and representatives throughout the world

ISBN 978 0 230 73483 8

Text © Emma Mohamed 2012
Design and illustration © Macmillan Publishers Limited 2012

First published 2012

All rights reserved; no part of this publication may be reproduced, stored in a retrieval system, transmitted in any form, or by any means, electronic, mechanical, photocopying, recording, or otherwise, without the prior written permission of the publishers.

Designed by Echelon Design
Illustrated by Kathy Baxendale, David Belmont (Beehive), Lee Carey, Grace Chen (Sylvie Poggio), Echelon Design, James Hart (Sylvie Poggio), John Haslam, Martin Impey, Nigel Kitching (Sylvie Poggio), Janette Louden, Paul McCaffrey (Sylvie Poggio), Eric Olsen (Sylvie Poggio)
Cover design by Echelon Design
Cover photos by Lisa Payne
Songs produced and arranged by Tom, Dick and Debbie Productions
Recordings produced and arranged by James Richardson
Pictures researched by Kevin Brown

These materials may contain links for third party websites. We have no control over, and are not responsible for, the contents of such third party websites. Please use care when accessing them.

Although we have tried to trace and contact copyright holders before publication, in some cases this has not been possible. If contacted we will be pleased to rectify any errors or omissions at the earliest opportunity.

Author's acknowledgments

I'd like to thank everyone at Macmillan Spain and Oxford for their help with the development of Quest 6. I'd like to thank the teachers I've worked with throughout the years, for their insights into teaching and for the many laughs shared in staff rooms. And finally, I'd like to thank my mum Sue, my little boy Danny, Jose Luis, Jeff and Dee for their encouragement and support.

Printed and bound in China

2016 2015 2014 2013
10 9 8 7 6 5 4 3 2

Acknowledgments

The publishers would like to thank the following teachers and schools:
Ana Visairas Blanco, Colegio Sagrado Corazón Jesuitas, Logroño, La Rioja; Conxi Rodrigo Niubo, Escola Pia Santa Anna, Mataró, Barcelona; Christine González Álvarez, CEIP Francisco de Quevedo, Majadahonda, Madrid; Dolors Verdugo Rangel, CEIP Puig d'Agulles, Corbera de Llobregat, Barcelona; Elena Sánchez Méndez, Colegio La Anunciata Ikastetxea, Pasai Antxo, Guipuzcoa; Esperanza Cervera, CEIP Lluís Vives, Massanassa, Valencia; J.Javier Martínez Izquierdo, CEIP Mariano José Larra, Madrid; Javier Sánchez Mir, Colegio Hermanos Maristas, Valencia; Mamen Ruiz de Gauna Montoya, Colegio Sagrado Corazón, Haro, La Rioja; María Ángeles Puga Zuccotti, CEIP Joaquín Turina, Madrid; Mariana Fernández Pellón, CEIP Marià Manent, Premià de Dalt, Barcelona; Mª Carmen Vilchez Lechuga, CEIP Ángel López Salazar, Baeza, Jaen; Mª Jesús Pérez González, CEIP Camilo José Cela, Madrid; Mª José Durán Ríos, Colegio Dulce Nombre de María PP Escolapios, Granada; Olivia Sánchez , CEIP Lluís Piquer, Paret del Vallès, Barcelona; Sara Oliva Martínez, CEIP Marià Manent, Premià de Dalt, Barcelona; Susana García Santos, Colegio Santa Ana, Zaragoza; Sylvia Frey Salcedo, CEIP La Cañada, Olías, Málaga.

The authors and publishers would like to thank the following for permission to reproduce their photographs:
Alamy/Kitch Bain pp8(3), 11(mat), Alamy/Phil Degginger pp1(6), 45(tr), Alamy/Li Ding p2(mask), Alamy/Greg Balfour Evans pp37(4), 43(4), Alamy/Andrew Fox pp37(10), 43(10), Alamy/Fresh Start Images pp13(7), 19(7), Alamy/Eric Gevaert p57(tr), Alamy/HINKS p16(l), Alamy/D.Hurst pp1(8), 61(tr), Alamy/Image Source p20(t), Alamy/IS2 from Image Source pp5(9), 11(5), Alamy/James Jackson p65(b), Alamy/Nigel James p33(r), Alamy/Kuttig People pp5(1), 11(1), Alamy/Norberto Lauria p33(l), Alamy/London Aerial Photo Library pp37(1), 43(1), Alamy/Lusoimages – Seasonal p61(10), 67(10), Alamy/Antony Nettle pp37(2), 43(2), Alamy/Paik Photography p65(tl), Alamy/Mike Robinson pp37(7), 43(7), Alamy/Charles Stirling pp37(9), 43(9), Alamy/Tetra Images pp61(4), 67(7), Alamy/Hugh Threlfall pp8(5), 11(fishing rod), 61(8), 67(10), Alamy/Adina Tovy p71(d), Alamy/Travel Pictures pp37(6), 43(6), Alamy/Andrew Twort p49(tr); **Art Directors & TRIP**/Helene Rogers pp3(sports bag), 13(1, 3, 8, 9, 10), 19(1, 3, 8, 9, 10), 49(tl), 61(5, 6), 67(3, 8), Art Directors & TRIP/Brian Vikander p60(t); **Bananastock** pp40(l, tr), 69(bl); Illustration © 2009 **Christian Birmingham** Reproduced by permission of Walker Books Ltd, London SE11 5HJ www.walker.co.uk p25(t); **Brand X Pictures** pp3(artist), 37(5, 8), 43(5, 8); **Bridgeman Art Library**/Gray Scramble (single),1969(acrylic on canvas) by Stella, Frank (b.1936) Private Collection/Mayor Gallery, London ©ARS, NY and DACS, London, 2011 p9(bl); **Pedro Campos** "Jelly Beans" Madrid 1966 (Oil on Canvas, 150x150cm) p9(tl); **Comstock Images** pp2(beans), 28(t); **Corbis** pp3(clown), 4(frame cr), 5(8), 11(9), 13(2), 17(tl), 19(2), 56(1, 3), 58(b, l), 59(1, 3) Corbis/Karl Ammann p 54(tl), Corbis/Atlantide Phototravel p2(tr), Corbis/Daniel Attia pp5(7), 11(4), Corbis/Bettmann p48(r), Corbis/Sam Forencich p41(bl), Corbis/Emma Foster/epa p50(b), Corbis/Fotofeeling/WestEnd p56(tr), Corbis/Jamie Grill/Tetra Images p16(r), Corbis/Martin Harvey pp56(2), 59(2), Corbis/John Henley/Blend Images pp5(6), 11(8), Corbis/Janssen/photocuisine pp29(10), 35(omelette), Corbis/Justin Lane/epa pp1(festivals c), 70(tr), Corbis/Paddy Lincks p12(t), Corbis/Gideon Mendel/In Pictures p71(b), Corbis/David Moir/X02060/Reuters p69(c), Corbis/Alessia Pierdomenico/Reuters pp1(festivals r), 71(a), Corbis/Rious/photocuisine pp29(9), 35(pancake), Corbis/Radius Images p61(7), 67(4), Corbis/Patrick Ward p71(c), Corbis/Julian Winslow pp5(3), 11(2); **DigitalStock**/Corbis pp41(t), 56(cr); **DK Images**/Howard Shooter pp13(6), 19(6); **FLPA – Images of Natures**/Gerry Ellis/Minden Pictures p56(br); **Grapheast** p44(t); **Getty Images** pp2(turtle), 4(frame cl), 29(6), 35(lemon), 65(tr), 68(t), 70(a), Getty Images/AFP p54(b), Getty Images/Steve Allen pp56(5), 59(5), Getty Images/Dorling Kindersley pp61(3), 67(2), Getty Images/EIGHTFISH pp1(3), 21(tr), Getty Images/Beth Galton pp1(4) 28(t), Getty Images/Steve Gorton pp16(2), 19(wool), Getty Images/Nicki Pardo pp61(1), 67(1), Getty Images/Photolibrary p69(d), Getty Images/Susanna Price p8(tc), Getty Images/John Rowley p42(b), Getty Images/Karen Su p57(tl), Getty Images/Julie Toy/FoodPix pp29(4), 35(salt), Getty Images/James Warwick p57(br), Getty Images/Mel Yates pp5(2), 11(6); **Glow Images** pp16(4), 19(denim), 29(5), 35(mango), Glow Images/Marcin Balcerzak p8(tr), Glow Images/Sylvie Bouchard pp1(2), 13(tr), Glow Images/Gita Kulinica pp29(8), 35(doughnut), Glow Images/Natalie Merzlyakova pp8(1), 11(paintbrush), Glow Images/Carlos Santa Maria pp1(festivals l), 69(tr), Glow Images/Vitaliy Shabalin pp8(2), 11(album), Glow Images/Bruce Shippee pp13(4), 19(4), Glow Images/Aleksey Telnov pp61(2), 67(6), Glow Images/Cathy Yeulet p33(c); **Photo courtesy of KK Gregory, and Wristies Inc** pp48(tc), 49(br); **Harper Collins Publishers Ltd**/©2002 CS Lewis p25(tl), Harper Collins Publishers Ltd/ ©2009 JRR Tolkien p25(bl); **iStockphoto** p1(1), p4(frame l), 5(cr); **Image 100** p56(4), 59(4); **Image Source** pp1(5), 4(frame r), 29(1, 3), 35(butter, sugar), 37(tr), 40(tc, bc); **Macmillan Australia** pp29(2), 35(milk), Macmillan Australia/Primary Library/Richard Morden p2(map); **Macmillan Publishers Ltd** p2(sunglasses), Macmillan Publishers Ltd/Paul Bricknell/Dean Ryan pp29(7), 35(flour); **Mary Evans Picture Library** p41(br); ©Julian Opie. All Rights Reserved, DACS 2011 p9(cr); **Photo Alto** pp16(5), 19(leather); **Photodisc** pp16(3), 19(silk); **Press Association Images**/PA Archive p49(bl); **Rex Features** pp5(4), 11(7), Rex Features/© 20th Century Fox/Everett pp24(l, r), Rex Features/Albanpix Ltd p6(b), Rex Features/Nigel R. Barklie pp37(3), 43(3), Rex Features/Tom Chance/WestEnd61 p32, Rex Features/Andrew Drysdale pp8(4), 11(cards), Rex Features/Richard Jones p36(t), Rex Features/McPix Ltd p17(c), Rex Features/Stephen Meddle p69(b), Rex Features/Geoff Moore p52(l), Rex Features/Bernd Nasner/Action Press p3(tl), Rex Features/Erik Pendzich pp8(br), 69(a), Rex Features/Claudia Rehm/WestEnd61 pp5(10), 11(10), Rex Features/Sipa Press pp8(bl, bc); **Science Photo Library**/Patrice Latron/Look At Sciences p17(r), Science Photo Library/Sheila Terry p48(l); **Superstock**/age fotostock pp1(7), 8(tl), 53(tl), Superstock/Clover pp16(1), 19(cotton), Superstock/Flirt p17(bl), Superstock/FoodCollection p3(peaches), Superstock/imagebroker.net p71(tr), Superstock/Space Images pp61(9), 67(5), Superstock/The Irish Collection p70(d).

Artist reference photos with thanks to: Corbis/Bettmann; Rex Features/Albanpix Ltd; Rex Features/Ken McKay.

Commissioned photography by Lisa Payne pp2(black top, boy, girl), 3(boy, girl), 4(l), 5(tl, br, 5), 6(tr), 7, 10, 11(3), 12(b), 13(br, 5), 14, 15, 18, 19(5), 20(b), 21(tl, br), 22, 23, 26, 28(b), 29(tl, br), 30, 31, 34, 36(b), 37(tl, br), 38, 39, 42(t), 44(b), 45(tl, br), 46, 47, 50(t), 52(b), 53(tl, br), 54(tr), 55, 58(t), 60(b), 61(tl, br), 62, 63, 66, 68(b), 69(tl), 70(t), 71(tl).
Thanks to Alabama, Denniel, Saffia, Tilly & Tom.
Front cover photos by **DigitalStock** (cl); **Image Source** (tl); **Lisa Payne** (main,bl).

Commissioned photographs by Lisa Payne

Thanks to Denniel, Isobel, Oliver, Saffia, Tilly & Tom.